Sun Kisses, Moon Hugs

By Susan Schaefer Bernardo ◆ Illustrated by Courtenay Fletcher

Inner Flower Child Books

Los Angeles

Inner Flower Child Books
17412 Ventura Blvd., Suite 134
Encino, CA 91316

Visit us on the web at www.sunkissesmoonhugs.com

First Edition: November 2012
ISBN 978-0-9711228-1-9 (hardcover)

The illustrations for this book were created digitally on a Mac.
The text was set in Phaistos Roman and Architect's Daughter.

Book design by Courtenay Fletcher

Printed and bound in the United States of America

Sealed with a kiss for Mom and Dad
and my sons Brendan and Charlie...
Guess what? You know what? I love you!

–S.B.

For Macallan, who puts rainbows in my heart each day...
and my mom, who taught me to hug the moon.

–C.F.

A million hugs and kisses
to our amazing community of family
and friends, old and new...
your support made this book possible.

xoxo Courtenay and Susan

No matter how far apart we are,
I'll always find ways to tell you I love you.

How?

From wherever we stand,

you see the moon and I see the moon.

That is how we

can send each other hugs.

Moon hugs?
Yes, moon hugs.

But the moon doesn't have any arms!

It's true the moon cannot reach down to hold your hand,
but she is strong enough to pull waves onto sand.

Her invisible arms rock the tides by night and day,
like my love holds you safely when I am away.

What if the moon is just a sliver?

Still she will deliver an entire quiver full of love.

However small and thin the moon might seem,

the hugs we send always make her beam.

What if there's no moon in sight?

Close your eyes and imagine it bright,

and love will dance in your dreams tonight.

But when I wake up, the moon will be gone!

Ahh, but then we can send each other kisses by dawn.

When you open your eyes and see the sun rise,

just do this... blow a kiss!

The sun will catch your kiss and use light speed, to forward it right on to me

I'll send a million kisses back your way. You'll feel my love in each warm ray.

But what if...

I know what you're about to say...what if the sky is cloudy or gray?

Love travels through raindrops and waters the ground,
flows into rivers and oceans all around.

When the sky clears and the sun joins the show,

our kisses, like wishes, will slide down rainbows.

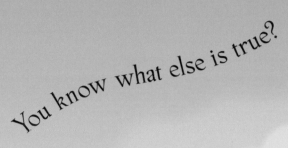

You know what else is true?

Every ladybug and butterfly,

each dandelion and daisy

that catches your eye or flutters by,

is saying that I'm crazy

about you.

From the heavens above to earth below,
there are infinite ways to say hello.
Love is in each star twinkling in space
and every frosty snowflake tickling your face.

Throw your arms around a tree...I'll hug you and you'll hug me.

Each grain of sand means I'm in reach

when you're playing on the beach.

I'm leaving signs to show I care, like the wind whispering through your hair.

Whenever I miss you,

I will find a way to hug and kiss you.

See these letters X and O?

They're another way for us to show

something forever true...

You love me, and I love you.

Hugs by moon and kisses by sun,

I'll always love you, Little One.

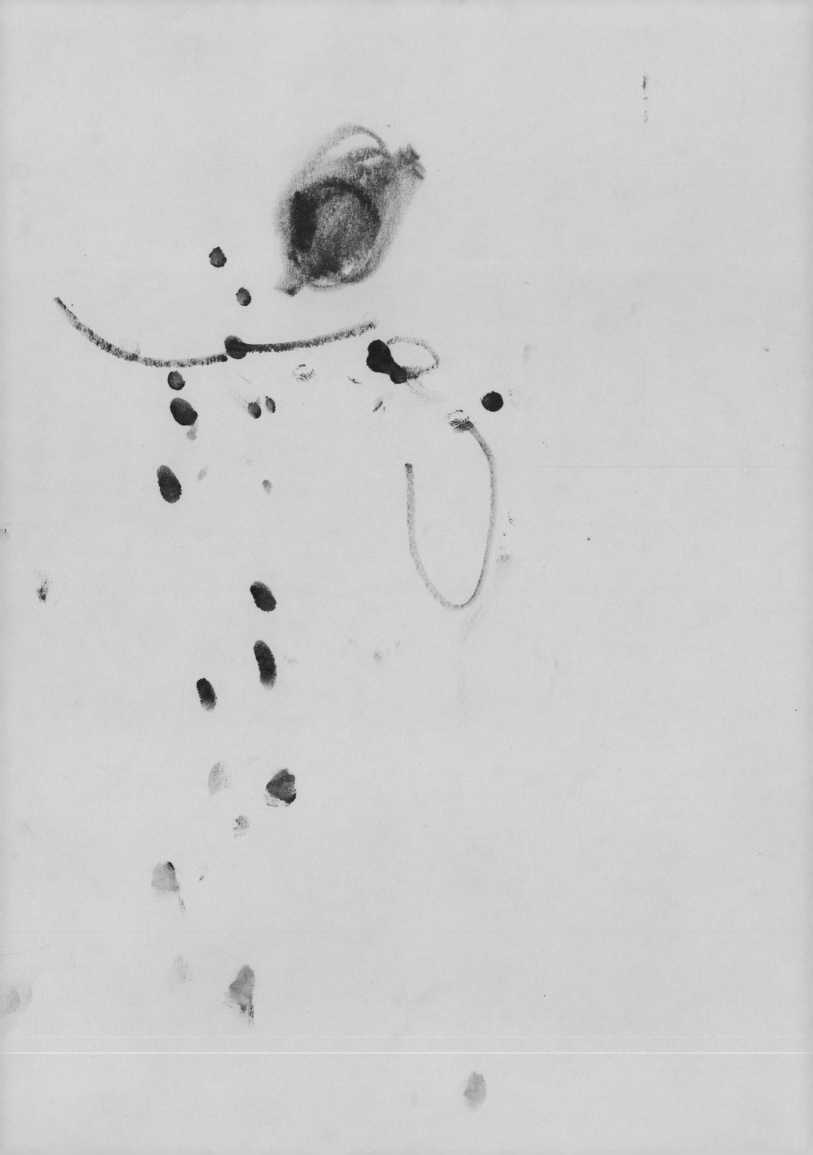